THE BASICS OF

FMEA

THE BASICS OF

FMEA

2nd Edition

Robin E. McDermott
Raymond J. Mikulak
Michael R. Beauregard

CRC Press
Taylor & Francis Group

A PRODUCTIVITY PRESS BOOK

Productivity Press
Taylor & Francis Group
270 Madison Avenue
New York, NY 10016

© 2009 by Taylor & Francis Group, LLC
Productivity Press is an imprint of Taylor & Francis Group, an Informa business

No claim to original U.S. Government works
Printed in the United States of America on acid-free paper
10 9 8 7 6 5 4 3 2 1

International Standard Book Number-13: 978-1-56327-377-3 (Softcover)

Visit the Taylor & Francis Web site at
http://www.taylorandfrancis.com

and the Productivity Press Web site at
http://www.productivitypress.com

Contents

Introduction

Failure Mode and Effect Analysis (FMEA) techniques have been around for over 40 years. It was only in the late twentieth century, however, that FMEAs gained widespread appeal outside the safety arena. This was thanks in large part to the U.S. automotive industry with its QS-9000 supplier requirements that were established in 1996 and global efforts by the International Automotive Task Force (IATF) to build on QS-9000 (and other international quality standards) with the development of ISO/TS 16949.

The 2002 revision of ISO/TS 16949 incorporates ISO 9001:2000 and defines the quality system requirements (and application of ISO 9001) for automotive production and relevant service part organizations.

The ISO/TS 16949 standard requires that suppliers to the automotive industry conduct product/design and process FMEAs in an effort to prevent failures before they happen.

Unlike many quality improvement tools, FMEAs do not require complicated statistics, yet they can yield significant savings for a company while at the same time reducing the potential costly liability of a process or product that does not perform as promised.

FMEAs do take time and people resources. Because FMEAs are team based, several people need to be involved in the process. The foundation of FMEAs is the FMEA team members and their input during the FMEA process. Companies must be prepared to allow the team enough time to do a thorough job. Effective FMEAs cannot be done by one person alone sitting in an office filling out the FMEA forms. Automotive customers and ISO auditors today can easily spot an FMEA that was done just to appease the customer and fulfill standards requirements.

This booklet was designed to help shorten the learning curve for FMEA teams and to help them conduct effective and efficient FMEAs, even if it is their very first FMEA. The book's easy-to-use reference format makes it an invaluable resource for FMEA teams.

Chapter 1

What Is an FMEA?

An FMEA (Failure Mode and Effect Analysis) is a systematic method of identifying and preventing product and process problems before they occur. FMEAs are focused on preventing defects, enhancing safety, and increasing customer satisfaction. Ideally, FMEAs are conducted in the product design or process development stages, although conducting an FMEA on existing products and processes can also yield substantial benefits.

The History of FMEAs

The first formal FMEAs were conducted in the aerospace industry in the mid-1960s and were specifically focused on safety issues. Before long, FMEAs became a key tool for improving safety, especially in the chemical process industries. The goal with safety FMEAs was, and remains today, to prevent safety accidents and incidents from occurring.

While engineers have always analyzed processes and products for potential failures, the FMEA process standardizes the approach and establishes a common language that can be used both within and between companies. It can also be used by nontechnical as well as technical employees of all levels.

The automotive industry adapted the FMEA technique for use as a quality improvement tool.

Chapter 2

What Is the Purpose of an FMEA?

Preventing process and product problems before they occur is the purpose of Failure Mode and Effect Analysis (FMEA). Used in both the design and manufacturing processes, they substantially reduce costs by identifying product and process improvements early in the develop process when changes are relatively easy and inexpensive to make. The result is a more robust process because the need for after-the-fact corrective action and late change crises are reduced or eliminated.

Part of a Comprehensive Quality System

A formal FMEA process should be a part of a comprehensive quality system. While FMEAs can be effectively used alone, a company will not get maximum benefit without systems to support conducting FMEAs and implementing improvements that are a result of the FMEAs. For example, one element of a comprehensive quality system is effective use of data and information. Without reliable product or process data the FMEA becomes a guessing game based on opinions rather than actual facts. The result may be that the FMEA team focuses on the wrong failure modes, missing significant opportunities to improve the failure modes that are the biggest problems. Another example that supports the need for a comprehensive quality system is documentation of procedures.

This is especially critical with a process FMEA. In the absence of documented procedures, people working in the process could be introducing significant variation into it by operating it slightly differently each time the process is run. In this case, the FMEA is aiming at a moving target because each time the process is run, it produces different results.

There are many different models for quality systems, including ISO 9000, ISO/TS 16949, and the Malcolm Baldrige National Quality Award. The best model for a company depends on the type of business, the requirements of the customers of the business, and the current quality systems that are already in place.

FMEAs and Bottom-Line Results

Effective use of FMEAs can have a positive impact on an organization's bottom line because of their preventive nature. Here are three real examples.

Example 1

Ford required a manufacturer of automobile liquid-level floats to conduct both a design/product FMEA and a process FMEA. The manufacturer established three FMEA teams, each tasked with a different aspect of the process/product. Three team leaders were assigned and were responsible for ensuring the team's efforts were coordinated.

The Results

- The combined efforts of the teams resulted in a decrease in defectives to 0.2 part per million.
- The equipment uptime increased from 74 percent to 89 percent.
- Customer complaints dropped from an average of two per year to none.
- Productivity per labor hour increased by 22 percent.

Example 2

An aircraft engine manufacturer conducted an FMEA on its engine assembly operation. A cross-functional team was formed that included individuals from outside of the assembly department, although all were familiar with assembly to some extent.

The Results

- The team identified the biggest risk of failure and mistake-proofed the process to the point where there was no chance of it recurring.
- Internal failures dropped to one-third of what they had been, eliminating problems that had existed for years but were not high enough a priority to address until the FMEA.
- The manufacturer saved $6,000 per month on engine teardowns.

Example 3

A small printed circuit board manufacturer with thirty-five employees formed an FMEA team. While the manager was a team member, his role was to keep notes, not to lead the team. After a brief FMEA training session, the team decided to collect data and information from other operators that were not on the team. With that information, they were able to complete the FMEA in four two-hour sessions.

The Results

- The highest-priority items were associated with the wave-soldering operation.
- The team discovered that many of the failure modes were related to preventive maintenance of the soldering unit.
- After establishing and implementing a preventive maintenance program, the team decreased solder defects on the complex boards they manufactured from an average of eleven per board to an average of one per board. The team continues to work to further reduce the defects.

Chapter 3

ISO 9000, ISO/TS 16949, and FMEAs

ISO 9000 is a family of standards for quality management systems.

When an organization achieves ISO 9000 certification, that organization has developed, instituted, and uses systems capable of controlling processes that determine the acceptability of its product or services. ISO 9001:2000, which combined the earlier standards of ISO 9001, 9002, and 9003, defines the requirements of a comprehensive quality management system.

ISO/TS 16949:2002 takes ISO 9001 one step further with an emphasis on a process approach. While ISO/TS 16949:2002 is based on ISO 9001, it contains complementary automotive industry-specific requirements adding to the standard both a process orientation and a focus on the customer.

Specific actions required to fulfill ISO are defined throughout the ISO/TS 16949 standard, particularly in Sections 5 ("Management Responsibility"), 6 ("Resource Management"), and 7 ("Product Realization"). Most of the references to FMEAs are in Section 7.

See Appendix 6 for a listing of FMEA-related references in ISO/TS 16949.

Chapter 4

The FMEA Process

The objective of an FMEA is to look for all of the ways a process or product can fail. A product failure occurs when the product does not function as it should or when it malfunctions in some way. Even the simplest products have many opportunities for failure. For example, a drip coffeemaker—a relatively simple household appliance—could have several things fail that would render the coffeemaker inoperable. Here are some possible ways the coffeemaker can fail:

- The heating element does not heat water to sufficient temperature to brew coffee.
- The pump does not pump water into the filter basket.
- The coffeemaker does not turn on automatically by the clock.
- The clock stops working or runs too fast or too slow.
- Calcium deposits from impure water clog up the brewing process.
- There is either not enough or too much coffee used.
- There is a short in the electrical cord.

Failures are not limited to problems with the product. Because failures also can occur when the user makes a mistake, those types of failures should also be included in the FMEA. Anything that can be done to ensure the product works correctly, regardless of how the user operates it, will move the product closer to 100 percent total customer satisfaction.

Ways in which a product or process can fail are called failure modes. Each failure mode has a potential effect, and some effects are more likely to occur than others. In addition, each potential effect has a relative risk associated with it. The FMEA process is a way to identify the failures, effects, and risks within a process or product, and then eliminate or reduce them.

Evaluating the Risk of Failure

The relative risk of a failure and its effects is determined by three factors:

- **Severity**—The consequence of the failure should it occur.
- **Occurrence**—The probability or frequency of the failure occurring.
- **Detection**—The probability of the failure being detected before the impact of the effect is realized.

Assessing the Risk Priority Number

Using the data and knowledge of the process or product, each potential failure mode and effect is rated in each of these three factors on a scale ranging from 1 to 10, low to high.

By multiplying the ranking for the three factors (severity × occurrence × detection), a risk priority number (RPN) will be determined for each potential failure mode and effect.

The risk priority number (which will range from 1 to 1,000 for each failure mode) is used to rank the need for corrective actions to eliminate or reduce the potential failure modes. Those failure modes with the highest RPNs should be attended to first, although special attention should be given when the severity ranking is high (9 or 10) regardless of the RPN.

Once corrective action has been taken, a new RPN for the failure is determined by reevaluating the severity, occurrence, and detection rankings. This new RPN is called the "resulting RPN." Improvement and corrective action must continue until the resulting RPN is at an acceptable level for all potential failure modes.

Chapter 5

The FMEA Team

Although one person typically is responsible for coordinating the FMEA process, all FMEA projects are team based. The purpose for an FMEA team is to bring a variety of perspectives and experiences to the project.

Because each FMEA is unique in dealing with different aspects of the product or process, FMEA teams are formed when needed and disbanded once the FMEA is complete. In fact, it would be inappropriate to establish a permanent FMEA team because the composition of the team is dictated by the specific task or objective. In cases where several FMEAs are needed to cover one process or product, it is good practice to have some overlap of members between the teams, but there also should be some members who serve on only one or two of the teams to ensure a fresh perspective of the potential problems and solutions.

FMEA Team Size

The best size for the team is usually four to six people, but the minimum number of people will be dictated by the number of areas that are affected by the FMEA. Each area (for example, manufacturing, engineering, maintenance, materials, and technical service) should be represented on the team. The customer of the process, whether internal or external to the organization, can add another unique perspective as well and should be considered for team membership.

FMEA Team Membership

It is helpful also to have people on the team who have different levels of familiarity with the product or process. Those who are most familiar with it will have valuable insights, but may overlook some of the most obvious potential problems. Those who are less familiar with the process or product will bring unbiased, objective ideas into the FMEA process. Be aware that those with an emotional investment in the process or product may be overly sensitive during the critiquing process and may become defensive. Deciding whether to include these emotionally invested people on the team must involve weighing the disadvantages against the advantages that their experience and knowledge will bring to the process.

FMEA Team Leader

An FMEA team leader should be appointed by management or selected by the team as soon as it is assembled. The team leader is responsible for coordinating the FMEA process, including:

■ Setting up and facilitating meetings
■ Ensuring the team has the necessary resources available
■ Making sure the team is progressing toward the completion of the FMEA

The team leader should not dominate the team and does not normally have the final word on team decisions. The team leader's role is more like that of a facilitator than a decision maker.

Arrangements should be made for someone to be responsible for taking meeting minutes and maintaining the FMEA records. The scribe's role is often rotated among all team members, except the team leader. This spreads the burden of recording the meeting equally among all participants.

The Role of the Process Expert

A point that is often debated with FMEAs is what role the process expert plays on the FMEA team. A person with expertise in the process (for example, the design engineer in a design FMEA or the process engineer in a process FMEA) can bring tremendous insight to the team and can help speed the process. In many ways he or she can be a real asset to the team. On the other hand, a process expert can also slow down the FMEA process.

An FMEA is a critical look at a product or process. People on the FMEA team who have a stake in the product or process being examined cannot allow their egos to get in the way of the FMEA. This is especially difficult for the process expert. Most likely he or she has a huge investment in the process or product, in terms of both time and personal integrity. The purpose of an FMEA, in essence, is to find flaws in that person's work. This can be a difficult process for an individual to go through and may result in several different types of reactions, including defensiveness, anger, and decreased self-esteem, all of which are counterproductive for both the team and process expert.

Training the FMEA Team

While it is helpful for FMEA team members to have some understanding of the FMEA process before starting the project (such as reading through this book and having it handy as a reference), extensive training is not necessary if team members have previous experience working on problem-solving teams. A team leader or facilitator who is well versed in the FMEA process can easily guide the team through the process as they are actually performing the FMEA. This means that there is not a need for extensive classroom training. Instead, the FMEA team can be immediately productive working on a real FMEA project and at the same time benefit from the most powerful form of training—experience.

It is important, however, that FMEA team members know the basics of working on a team because they will be using those skills as FMEA team members. Knowledge of consensus-building techniques, team project documentation, and idea-generating techniques such as brainstorming are all necessary for FMEA team members. In addition, team members should be comfortable using continuous-improvement problem-solving tools, such as flowcharts, data analysis, and graphing techniques.

Chapter 6

FMEA Boundaries of Freedom

It is important that the FMEA team has clearly defined boundaries within which they are free to conduct the FMEA and suggest and implement improvements. For example:

- Is the team responsible only for conducting the analysis, are they to make recommendations for improvements, and/or are they to implement the improvements?
- What is their spending budget?
- What other resources do they have at their disposal?
- Does the team face a deadline or other time constraints?
- What process must they follow if they need to expand beyond the defined boundaries?
- What and how should they communicate the FMEA process and results to others in the organization?

Management is responsible for defining the boundaries of freedom. Some of the boundaries of freedom can be standing guidelines for all FMEA teams. For example, a standard procedure can be established to define the process that teams must follow if they need to go beyond the normal boundaries, and this procedure can apply to all FMEA teams. The same holds true for the process that the team should use to communicate the FMEA results to others in the organization. Other boundaries will need to be set for each FMEA and will depend on the type of FMEA (design/product or process), the scope of the FMEA, and the people on the FMEA team.

While management is responsible for defining the boundaries of freedom, the FMEA team members have equal responsibility in making sure these boundaries are defined before the project gets under way. If the team members do not know what the boundaries are or if they are unclear about any of the boundaries, they should get clarification before proceeding with the FMEA. This will help the team avoid problems and conflicts later in the process.

FMEA Scope

The scope of the FMEA must be well defined. This definition usually comes from the leader of the function responsible for the FMEA. If the FMEA is focused on the design of a product, the head of the design function should clearly define the scope of the project. For a process FMEA, the leader of the manufacturing or manufacturing-engineering function would most likely define the scope.

A specific and clear definition of the process or product to be studied should be written and understood by everyone on the team. Team members should have an opportunity to clarify their understanding of the scope, if necessary, and those clarifications should be documented. This will help prevent the team from focusing on the wrong aspect of the product or process during the FMEA.

For example, if your team is working on a product FMEA for a new drip coffeemaker that your company has just developed, your definition of the product to be studied might be:

> Our team will conduct an FMEA on the new RS-100 coffeemaker and the glass carafe for that coffeemaker. The FMEA will not include any parts of this coffeemaker that are common to other coffeemakers in our product line, such as the electronic clock, the electrical cord and wiring into the coffeemaker, and the gold cone coffee filter.

A specific and clear definition is even more important with process FMEAs because they can encompass so many different aspects of the process manufacturing chain, from the raw materials to components, to the actual manufacturing and assembly, to the shipping, and everything in between. While each part of the chain plays an important role in the quality of a product, it may help to use a narrow definition of the process to ensure that the FMEA project is completed in a timely manner.

Because large processes may be difficult to work on in their entirety, break them into subprocesses when possible and attend to them one at a time, or have several teams working at the same time on different subprocesses.

FMEA Team Start-Up Worksheet		
FMEA Number: _____	Date Started: _____	
Team Members: _____	Date Completed: _____ _____	_____ _____
_____	_____	_____
Leader: _____		
Who will take minutes and maintain records?	_____	
1. What is the scope of the FMEA? Include a clear definition of the process (PFMEA) or product (DFMEA) to be studied. (Attach the Scope Worksheet.)		
2. Are all affected areas represented? (circle one)		
YES NO	Action: _____	
3. Are different levels and types of knowledge represented on the team? (circle one)		
YES NO	Action: _____	
4. Are customers or suppliers involved? (circle one)		
YES NO	Action: _____	
Boundaries of Freedom		
5. What aspect of the FMEA is the team responsible for? (circle one)		
FMEA Analysis	Recommendations for Improvement	Implementation of Improvements
6. What is the budget for the FMEA?	_____	
7. Does the project have a deadline?	_____	
8. Do team members have specific time constraints?	_____	
9. What is the procedure if the team needs to expand beyond these boundaries?	_____	
10. How should the FMEA be communicated to others?	_____	

Figure 6.1   FMEA Team Start-Up Worksheet.

FMEA Start-Up Worksheet

The FMEA Start-Up Worksheet, shown in Figure 6.1, can help the members of a team make sure they have a clear understanding of their boundaries of freedom and their roles and responsibilities before the project gets under way.

Chapter 7

Product/Design versus Process FMEAs

The principles and steps behind all FMEAs, whether they are focused on the product or the process, are the same even though the objectives may differ.

Product/Design

- The objective for a product or design FMEA is to uncover problems with the product that will result in safety hazards, product malfunctions, or a shortened product life. As consumers, we are all too familiar with examples of these types of problems, such as an air bag in a car that may not work properly or a paint job that cracks and dulls within the first three or four years that you own the car.
- Product FMEAs can be conducted at each phase in the design process (preliminary design, prototype, or final design), or they can be used on products that are already in production. The key question asked in design FMEAs is: How can the product fail?
- See Figure 7.1 for a sample worksheet for defining the scope of a design FMEA study.

Design FMEA Scope Worksheet		
Product:	Date:	Scope defined by:
Part 1: Who is the customer?		
Part 2: What are the product features and characteristics?		
Part 3: What are the product benefits?		
Part 4: Study the entire product or only components or subassemblies?		
Part 5: Include consideration of raw material failures?		
Part 6: Include packaging, storage, and transit?		
Part 7: What are the operational process requirements and constraints?		

Figure 7.1 Design FMEA Scope Worksheet.

Process

- Process FMEAs uncover process problems related to the manufacture of the product. For example, a piece of automated assembly equipment may misfeed parts, resulting in products not being assembled correctly. Or, in a chemical manufacturing process, temperature and mixing time could be sources of potential failures, resulting in an unusable product.
- It is helpful when conducting a process FMEA to think in terms of the five elements of a process: people, materials, equipment, methods, and environment. With these five elements in mind, ask: How can process failure affect the product, processing efficiency, or safety?
- See Figure 7.2 for a sample worksheet for defining the scope of a process FMEA study.

Process FMEA Scope Worksheet		
Process:	Date:	Scope defined by:
Part 1: What process components are to be included in the investigation?		
Part 2: Who is the customer?		
Part 3: What process support systems are to be included in the study?		
Part 4: To what extent should input materials be studied?		
Part 5: What are the product material requirements and constraints?		
Part 6: Should packaging, storage and transit be considered part of this study?		

Figure 7.2   Process FMEA Scope Worksheet.

Both types of FMEAs use severity, occurrence, and detection rankings, although the definitions of the ranking scale for each may be different. Many organizations have different customized ranking scales for their product FMEAs and process FMEAs. The ranking scales presented in this book are suggestions and can be used as starting points to develop customized ranking scales specifically designed for a particular organization.

Chapter 8

Ten Steps for an FMEA

All product/design and process FMEAs follow these ten steps:

Table 8.1   10 Steps for an FMEA

Step 1	Review the process or product.
Step 2	Brainstorm potential failure modes.
Step 3	List potential effects of each failure mode.
Step 4	Assign a severity ranking for each effect.
Step 5	Assign an occurrence ranking for each failure mode.
Step 6	Assign a detection ranking for each failure mode and/or effect.
Step 7	Calculate the risk priority number for each effect.
Step 8	Prioritize the failure modes for action.
Step 9	Take action to eliminate or reduce the high-risk failure modes.
Step 10	Calculate the resulting RPN as the failure modes are reduced or eliminated.

These steps are explained in detail following the FMEA worksheet section and are illustrated in a case study.

The FMEA Worksheet

The FMEA process should be documented using an FMEA worksheet (see Figure 8.1). This form captures all of the important information about the FMEA and serves as an excellent communication tool. Alternative workshop formats for Design FMEAs and Process FMEAs can be found in Appendix 7.

Line	Component and Function	Potential Failure Mode	Potential Effect(s) of Failure	Severity	Potential Cause(s) of Failure	Occurrence	Current Controls, Prevention	Current Controls, Detection	Detection	RPN	Recommended Action	Responsibility and Target Completion Date	Action Taken	Severity	Occurrence	Detection	RPN
1																	
2																	
3																	
4																	
5																	
6																	
7																	
8																	
9																	
10																	

Failure Mode and Effects Analysis Worksheet

Process or Product: _____
FMEA Team: _____
Team Leader: _____

FMEA Date: (Original) _____
(Revised) _____
FMEA Number: _____
Page: 1 of 1

FMEA Process

Action Results

Figure 8.1 Blank FMEA Worksheet.

Some organizations have their own format for the FMEA worksheet. Others will adapt this form to meet their needs.

The worksheet is easiest to work with when enlarged to 11 × 17 inches in size or when put on to a large poster or projected from a computer for use during the team meeting.

A numbering system to track and access FMEA previously conducted projects is helpful. The numbering system should enable cross-referencing to similar FMEAs as well as other improvement activities dealing with the same product or process.

Copies of all FMEAs should be kept in a central location so they are easily accessible during audits or internal process and product reviews.

Step 1: Review the Process or Product

The team should review a blueprint (or engineering drawing) of the product if they are considering a product FMEA or a detailed flowchart of the operation if they are conducting a process FMEA. This will help ensure that everyone on the FMEA team has the same understanding of the product or process that is being worked on.

If a blueprint or flowchart is not available, the team will need to create one prior to starting the FMEA process. (Information on creating a flowchart can be found in Appendix 1.)

With the blueprint or flowchart in hand, the team members should familiarize themselves with the product or process. For a product FMEA, they should physically see the product or a prototype of it. For a process FMEA, the team should physically walk through the process exactly as the process flows.

It is helpful to have an "expert" on the product or process available to answer any questions the team might have.

Step 2: Brainstorm Potential Failure Modes

Once everyone on the team has an understanding of the process (or product), team members can begin thinking about potential failure modes that could affect the manufacturing process or the product quality. A brainstorming session will get all of those ideas out on the table. Team members should come to the brainstorming meeting with a list of their ideas. In addition to the ideas members bring to the meeting, others will be generated as a result of the synergy of the group process.

Because of the complexity of most manufactured products and manufacturing processes, it is best to conduct a series of brainstorming sessions, each focused on a different element (i.e., people, methods, equipment, materials, and the environment) of the product or process. Focusing on the elements one at a time will result in a more thorough list of potential failure modes.

It is not unusual to generate dozens of ideas from the brainstorming process. In fact, that is the objective!

Once the brainstorming is complete, the ideas should be organized by grouping them into like categories. Your team must decide the best categories for grouping, as there are many different ways to group failure modes. You can group them by the type of failure (e.g., electrical, mechanical, user created), where on the product or process the failure occurs, or the seriousness (at least the team's best guess at this point) of the failure. Grouping the failures will make the FMEA process easier to work through. Without the grouping step, the team may invest a lot of energy jumping from one aspect of the product to a completely different aspect of the product and then back again. An easy way to work through the grouping process is to put all of the failure modes onto self-stick notes and post them on a wall so they are easy to see and move around as they are being grouped.

The grouping also gives the team a chance to consider whether some failure modes should be combined, because they are the same or very similar to each other. When the failure modes have been grouped and combined, if appropriate, they should be transferred onto the FMEA sheet. The example in Figure 8.2 shows how each component (part of the process or piece of the product) and its intended function are listed, and next to each you can see the potential failure modes associated with each item. Note that there are usually several failure modes for each component.

Step 3: List Potential Effects for Each Failure Mode

With the failure modes listed on the FMEA Worksheet, the FMEA team reviews each failure mode and identifies the potential effects of the failure should it occur. For some of the failure modes, there may be only one effect, while for other modes there may be several effects.

This step must be thorough because this information will feed into the assignment of risk rankings for each of the failures. It is helpful to think of this step as an if-then process: *If* the failure occurs, *then* what are the consequences?

Steps 4–6: Assigning Severity, Occurrence, and Detection Rankings

Each of these three rankings is based on a 10-point scale, with 1 being the lowest ranking and 10 the highest.

Line	Component and Function	Potential Failure Mode	Potential Effect(s) of Failure	Severity	Potential Cause(s) of Failure	Occurrence	Current Controls, Prevention
			Failure Mode and Effects A|				
	Process or Product: Product: Model X-1050 Fire Extinguisher						
	FMEA Team: Kevin M, Shane T, KC McG, Chase L, Tyler J						
	Team Leader: Kevin M.						
			FMEA Process				
1	Hose; delivers extinguishing agent	Cracks					
2		Pinholes					
3		Blockages					
4	Canister; reservoir for extinguishing agent	Paint coverage uneven					
5		Canister dented					
6		Label not properly applied					
7	Charge gauge: determine remaining volume of agent	Inaccurate reading					
8		Broken crystal					
9	Valve mechanism; releases agent	Safety pin missing					
10		Handle jams					

Figure 8.2 Partially completed FMEA Worksheet.

It is important to establish clear and concise descriptions for the points on each of the scales, so that all team members have the same understanding of the rankings. The scales should be established before the team begins the ranking process. The more descriptive the team is when defining the ranking scale, the easier it should be to reach consensus during the ranking process.

A generic ranking system for each of the scales is provided in Tables 8.2 through 8.4. Note that in the generic example scales there is a scale for design FMEAs and one for process FMEAs for each of the three rankings of severity,

Table 8.2a (Generic) Design FMEA Severity Evaluation Criteria

Effect	Criteria: Severity of Effect on Product (Customer Effect)	Rank
Failure to Meet Safety and/or Regulatory Requirements	Potential failure mode affects safe vehicle operation and/or involves noncompliance with government regulations without warning.	10
	Potential failure mode affects safe vehicle operation and/or involves noncompliance with government regulations with warning.	9
Loss or Degradation of Primary Function	Loss of primary function (vehicle inoperable, does not affect safe vehicle operation).	8
	Degradation of primary function (vehicle operable, but at reduced level of performance).	7
Loss or Degradation of Secondary Function	Loss of primary function (vehicle inoperable, but comfort/ convenience functions inoperable).	6
	Degradation of primary function (vehicle inoperable, but comfort/ convenience functions at reduced level of performance).	5
Annoyance	Appearance or Audible Noise, vehicle operable, item does not conform and noticed by most customers (>75%).	4
	Appearance or Audible Noise, vehicle operable, item does not conform and noticed by many customers (50%).	3
	Appearance or Audible Noise, vehicle operable, item does not conform and noticed by discriminating customers (<25%).	2
No effect	No discernible effect.	1

Source: Reprinted from Potential Failure Mode and Effects Analysis, (FMEA 4th edition, 2008 Manual) with permission of DaimlerChrysler, Ford and GM Supplier Quality Requirements Task Force.

Table 8.2b   (Generic) Process FMEA Severity Evaluation Criteria

Effect	Criteria: Severity of Effect on Product (Customer Effect)	Rank	Effect	Criteria: Severity of Effect on Process (Manufacturing/Assembly Effect)
Failure to Meet Safety and/or Regulatory Requirements	Potential failure mode affects safe vehicle operation and/or involves noncompliance with government regulations without warning.	10	Failure to Meet Safety and/or Regulatory Requirements	May endanger operator (machine or assembly) without warning.
	Potential failure mode affects safe vehicle operation and/or involves noncompliance with government regulations with warning.	9		May endanger operator (machine or assembly) with warning.
Loss or Degradation of Primary Function	Loss of primary function (vehicle inoperable, does not affect safe vehicle operation).	8	Major Disruption	100% of product may have to be scrapped. Line shutdown or stop ship.
	Degradation of primary function (vehicle operable, but at reduced level of performance).	7	Significant Disruption	A portion of the production run may have to be scrapped. Deviation from primary process including decreased line speed or added manpower.
Loss or Degradation of Secondary Function	Loss of secondary function (vehicle inoperable but comfort/convenience functions inoperable).	6	Moderate Disruption	100% of production run may have to be reworked off line and accepted.
	Degradation of secondary function (vehicle inoperable but comfort/convenience functions at a reduced level of performance).	5		A portion of the production run may have to be reworked off line and accepted.
Annoyance	Appearance or Audible Noise, vehicle operable, item does not conform and noticed by most customers (>75%).	4	Moderate Disruption	100% of production run may have to be reworked in-station before it is processed.
	Appearance or Audible Noise, vehicle operable, item does not conform and noticed by many customers (50%).	3	Disruption	A portion of the production run may have to be reworked in-station before it is processed.
	Appearance or Audible Noise, vehicle operable, item does not conform and noticed by discriminating customers (<25%).	2	Minor Disruption	Slight inconvenience to process, operation, or operator
No effect	No discernible effect.	1	No effect	No discernible effect.

Source: Reprinted from Potential Failure Mode and Effects Analysis, (FMEA 4th edition, 2008 Manual) with permission of DaimlerChrysler, Ford and GM Supplier Quality Requirements Task Force.

Table 8.3a   (Generic) Design FMEA Occurrence Evaluation Criteria

Likelihood of Failure	Criteria: Occurrence of Causes – DFMEA (Design life/reliability of item/vehicle)	Incidents per item/vehicle	Rank
Very High	New technology/new design with no history.	≥100 per thousand ≥1 in 10	10
High	Failure is inevitable with new design, new application, or change in duty cycle/operating conditions.	50 per thousand 1 in 20	9
	Failure is likely with new design, new application, or change in duty cycle/operating conditions.	20 per thousand 1 in 50	8
	Failure is uncertain with new design, new application, or change in duty cycle/operating conditions.	10 per thousand 1 in 100	7
Moderate	Frequent failures associated with similar designs or in design simulation and testing.	2 per thousand 1 in 500	6
	Occasional failures associated with similar designs or in design simulation and testing.	0.5 per thousand 1 in 2,000	5
	Isolated failures associated with similar designs or in design simulation and testing.	0.1 per thousand 1 in 10,000	4
Low	Only isolated failures associated with almost identical design or in design simulation and testing.	0.01 per thousand 1 in 100,000	3
	No observed failures associated with almost identical design or in design simulation and testing.	≤0.001 per thousand 1 in 1,000,000	2
Very Low	Failure is eliminated through preventive control	Failure is eliminated through preventive control.	1

Source: Reprinted from Potential Failure Mode and Effects Analysis, (FMEA 4th edition, 2008 Manual) with permission of DaimlerChrysler, Ford and GM Supplier Quality Requirements Task Force.

Table 8.3b (Generic) Process FMEA Occurrence Evaluation Criteria

Likelihood of Failure	Criteria: Occurrence of Causes – DFMEA Incidents per item/vehicle	Rank
Very High	≥ 100 per thousand ≥ 1 in 10	10
High	50 per thousand 1 in 20	9
	20 per thousand 1 in 50	8
	10 per thousand 1 in 100	7
Moderate	2 per thousand 1 in 500	6
	0.5 per thousand 1 in 2,000	5
	0.1 per thousand 1 in 10,000	4
Low	0.01 per thousand 1 in 100,000	3
	≤0.001 per thousand 1 in 1,000,000	2
Very Low	Failure is eliminated through preventive control	1

Source: Reprinted from Potential Failure Mode and Effects Analysis, (FMEA 4th edition, 2008 Manual) with permission of DaimlerChrysler, Ford and GM Supplier Quality Requirements Task Force.

occurrence, and detection. This system should be customized by the organization for use with all FMEAs. See Appendix 4 for examples of custom ranking scales. The value of having one common set of ranking scales throughout an organization is that the rankings and the resulting risk priority numbers between FMEAs have a relationship to each other. This allows the organization to compare RPNs between FMEAs to further prioritize improvement activities.

Even if the ranking system is clear and concise, there still may be disagreement about the ranking for a particular item. In these cases, the techniques described in Appendix 3 may help the group reach consensus.

Step 4: Assign a Severity Ranking for Each Effect

The severity ranking is an estimation of how serious the effects would be if a given failure did occur. In some cases it is clear, because of past experience, how serious the problem would be. In other cases, it is necessary to estimate the severity based on the knowledge and expertise of the team members.

Table 8.4a (Generic) Design FMEA Prevention/Detection Evaluation Criteria

Opportunity for Detection	Criteria: Likelihood of Detection by Design Control	Rank	Likelihood of Detection
No detection opportunity	No current design control; Cannot detect or is not analyzed.	10	Almost Impossible
Not likely to detect at any stage	Design analysis/detection controls have a weak detection capability; Virtual Analysis (e.g., CAE, FEA, etc.) is **not correlated** to expected actual operating conditions.	9	Very Remote
	Product verification/validation after design freeze and prior to launch with **pass/fail** testing (Subsystem or system testing with acceptance criteria such as ride and handling, shipping evaluation, etc.).	8	Remote
Post Design Freeze and prior to launch	Product verification/validation after design freeze and prior to launch with **test to failure** testing (Subsystem or system testing until failure occurs, testing of system interactions, etc.).	7	Very Low
	Product verification/validation after design freeze and prior to launch with **degradation** testing (Subsystem or system testing after durability test, e.g., function check).	6	Low

		Description	Category
Moderate	5	Product validation (reliability testing, development or validation tests) prior to design freeze using **pass/fail** testing (e.g., acceptance criteria for performance, function checks, etc.).	Prior to Design Freeze
Moderately High	4	Product validation (reliability testing, development or validation tests) prior to design freeze using **test to failure** (e.g., until leaks, yields, cracks, etc.).	
High	3	Product validation (reliability testing, development or validation tests) prior to design freeze using **degradation** testing (e.g., data trends, before/after values, etc.).	
Very High	2	Design analysis/detection controls have a strong detection capability; Virtual Analysis (e.g., CAE, FEA, etc.) **is highly correlated** with actual or expected operating conditions prior to design freeze.	Virtual Analysis – Correlated
Almost Certain	1	Failure cause or failure mode cannot occur because it is fully prevented through design solutions (e.g., proven design standard, best practice or common material, etc.).	Detection not applicable; Failure Prevention

Source: Reprinted from Potential Failure Mode and Effects Analysis, (FMEA 4th edition, 2008 Manual) with permission of DaimlerChrysler, Ford and GM Supplier Quality Requirements Task Force.

Table 8.4b (Generic) Process FMEA Detection Evaluation Criteria

Opportunity for Detection	Criteria: Likelihood of Detection by Process Control	Rank	Likelihood of Detection
No detection opportunity	No current process control; Cannot detect or is not analyzed.	10	Almost Impossible
Not likely to detect at any stage	Failure Mode and/or Error (Cause) is not easily detected (e.g., random audits).	9	Very Remote
Problem Detection Post Processing	Failure Mode detection post-processing by operator through visual/tactile/audible means.	8	Remote
Problem Detection at Source	Failure Mode detection in-station by operator through visual/tactile/audible means or post-processing through use of attribute gauging (go/no-go, manual torque check/clicker wrench, etc.).	7	Very Low
Problem Detection Post Processing	Failure Mode detection post-processing by operator through use of variable gauging or in-station by operator through use of attribute gauging (go/no-go, manual torque check/clicker wrench, etc.).	6	Low
Problem Detection at Source	Failure Mode or Error (Cause) detection in-station by operator through the use of variable gauging or by automated controls in-station that will detect discrepant part and notify operator (light, buzzer, etc.). Gauging performed on setup and first-piece check (for set-up causes only.)	5	Moderate

Problem Detection Post Processing	Failure Mode detection post-processing by automated controls that will detect discrepant part and lock part to prevent further processing.		4	**Moderately High**
Problem Detection at Source	Failure Mode detection in-station by automated controls that will detect discrepant part and automatically lock part in station to prevent further processing.		3	**High**
Error Detection and/or Problem Prevention	Error (Cause) detection in-station by automated controls that will detect error and prevent discrepant part from being made.		2	**Very High**
Detection not applicable; Error Prevention	Error (Cause) prevention as a result of fixture design, machine design or part design. Discrepant parts cannot be made because item has been error-proofed by process/product design.		1	**Almost Certain**

Source: Reprinted from Potential Failure Mode and Effects Analysis, (FMEA 4th edition, 2008 Manual) with permission of DaimlerChrysler, Ford and GM Supplier Quality Requirements Task Force.

It is important to note that because each failure may have several different effects, and each effect can have a different level of severity. *It is the effect, not the failure*, which is rated. Therefore, each effect should be given its own severity ranking, even if there are several effects for a single failure mode.

Step 5: Assign an Occurrence Ranking for Each Failure Mode

The best method for determining the occurrence ranking is to use actual data from the process. This may be in the form of failure logs or even process capability data. When actual failure data are not available, the team must estimate how often a failure mode may occur. The team can make a better estimate of how likely a failure mode is to occur and at what frequency by knowing the potential cause of failure. Once the potential causes have been identified for all of the failure modes, an occurrence ranking can be assigned even if failure data do not exist.

Step 6: Assign a Detection Ranking for Each Failure Mode and/or Effect

The detection ranking looks at how likely we are to detect a failure or the effect of a failure. We start this step by identifying current controls that may detect a failure or effect of a failure. If there are no current controls, the likelihood of detection will be low, and the item would receive a high ranking, such as a 9 or 10. First, the current controls should be listed for all of the failure modes, or the effects of the failures, and then the detection rankings assigned.

Step 7: Calculate the Risk Priority Number for Each Failure Mode

The risk priority number (RPN) is simply calculated by multiplying the severity ranking times the occurrence ranking times the detection ranking for each item.

$$\text{Risk Priority Number} = \text{Severity} \times \text{Occurrence} \times \text{Detection}$$

The total risk priority number should be calculated by adding all of the risk priority numbers. This number alone is meaningless because each FMEA has a different number of failure modes and effects. However, it can serve as a gauge to compare the revised total RPN once the recommended actions have been instituted.

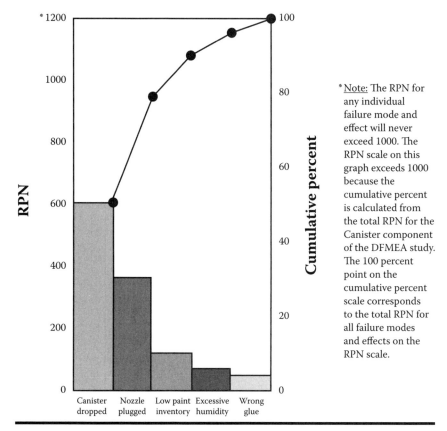

Figure 8.3 Pareto diagram of rankings.

* Note: The RPN for any individual failure mode and effect will never exceed 1000. The RPN scale on this graph exceeds 1000 because the cumulative percent is calculated from the total RPN for the Canister component of the DFMEA study. The 100 percent point on the cumulative percent scale corresponds to the total RPN for all failure modes and effects on the RPN scale.

Step 8: Prioritize the Failure Modes for Action

The failure modes can now be prioritized by ranking them in order, from the highest risk priority number to the lowest. Chances are that you will find that the 80/20 rule applies with the RPNs, just as it does with other quality improvement opportunities. In the case of the RPN, a literal translation would mean that 80 percent of the total RPN for the FMEA comes from just 20 percent of the potential failures and effects. A Pareto diagram (see Figure 8.3) is helpful to visualize the differences between the rankings for the failures and effects.

The team must now decide which items to work on. Usually it helps to set a cutoff RPN, where any failure modes with an RPN above that point are attended to. Those below the cutoff are left alone for the time being. For example, an organization may decide that any RPN above 200 creates an unacceptable risk. This decision sets the cutoff RPN at 200.

Step 9: Take Action to Eliminate or Reduce the High-Risk Failure Modes

Using an organized problem-solving process, identify and implement actions to eliminate or reduce the high-risk failure modes.

Ideally, the failure modes should be eliminated completely. For example, gasoline companies, car manufacturers, and pump manufacturers worked together during the phase-out of leaded fuel to eliminate the potential failure mode of putting leaded fuel into a car that runs on unleaded fuel. This was accomplished by making the gas tank opening too small for the leaded gas nozzle.

When a failure mode has been eliminated completely, the new risk priority number approaches zero because the occurrence ranking becomes one.

While elimination of failure modes altogether is ideal, it may not be achievable in all cases. When this happens, it helps to refer back to the severity, occurrence, and detection rankings that the team assigned to each item. Think of ways to reduce the rankings on one, two, or all three of the scales.

Often, the easiest approach for making a process or product improvement is to increase the detectability of the failure, thus lowering the detection ranking. For example, a coffeemaker might have a tone that sounds every ten minutes to remind you that it is turned on and that you need to turn it off before you leave the house, or a computer manufacturer may include a piece of software that notifies the user that there is low disk space.

However, these are Band-Aid approaches that often are costly and do not actually improve the quality of the product. Increasing failure detectability will simply make it easier to detect failures once they occur.

Reducing the severity is important, especially in situations that can lead to injuries. For example, a company that manufactures weed wackers might limit the speed of the machine, reducing the severity of a potential personal injury. However, the richest opportunity for improvement lies in reducing the likelihood of occurrence of the failure. After all, if it is highly unlikely that a failure will occur, there is less need for detection measures.

Table 8.5 identifies specific actions that can be taken to reduce the severity, occurrence, and detection rankings.

Step 10: Calculate the Resulting RPN as the Failure Modes Are Reduced

Once action has been taken to improve the product or process, new rankings for severity, occurrence, and detection should be determined, and a resulting RPN calculated.

Table 8.5   Specific Actions to Reduce Rankings

Severity	Occurrence	Detection
■ Personal protective equipment (e.g., hard hats or bump caps, side shields on safety glasses, full face protection, cut-proof gloves, long gloves) ■ Safety stops/emergency shut-offs ■ Use different material, such as safety glass that will not cause as severe an injury should it fail.	■ Increasing the Cpk through design of experiments and/or equipment modifications. ■ Focus on continuous improvement/ problem-solving teams. ■ Engaging mechanism that must be activated for the product or process work (e.g., some lawn mowers have handles that must be squeezed in order for them to operate).	■ Statistical process control (to monitor the process and identify when the process is going out of control) ■ Ensure the measuring devices are accurate and regularly calibrated. ■ Institute preventive maintenance to detect problems before they occur. ■ Use coding such as colors and shapes to alert the user or worker that something is either right or wrong.

For the failure modes where action was taken, there should be a significant reduction in the RPN. If not, that means action did not reduce the severity, likelihood of occurrence, or detectability.

The resulting RPNs can be organized on a Pareto diagram and compared with the original RPNs. In addition, the total RPNs of the before-and-after product or process can be compared and contrasted. You should expect at least a 50 percent or greater reduction in the total RPN after an FMEA.

There is no target RPN for FMEAs. It is up to the FMEA team and the company to decide on how far the team should go with improvements.

There will always be the potential for failure modes to occur. The question the company must ask is how much relative risk the team is willing to take. That answer will depend on the industry and the seriousness of failure. For example, in the nuclear industry, there is little margin for error; they cannot risk a disaster occurring. In other industries, it may be acceptable to take higher risks. If the team is satisfied with the resulting RPN, it should present the FMEA results to management, who will determine if additional work should be done to further reduce the RPNs.

Chapter 9

FMEA Case Study

This example of a design/product FMEA involves a manufacturer of fire extinguishers. The company developed a new extinguisher for home use. It wanted to make sure the extinguisher would be effective and would not cause any problems when used. The consequences of a faulty extinguisher could be life-threatening.

A team of five employees was formed to work through the FMEA process. The team included a design engineer who helped develop the extinguisher, the second-shift manufacturing supervisor, the first-shift quality technician, the purchasing manager, and the sales and marketing manager. The design engineer was appointed the team leader, and the members decided to name their team the "Fire Extinguisher FMEA Team."

The team boundaries were to complete the FMEA, including making improvements. The team was given a $5,000 budget and could request help from within the company to tap into outside team members' expertise. The deadline for project completion was April 15, at which time another team would be formed to conduct a process FMEA.

Case Study Step 1: Review the Process

All team members were given a blueprint of the fire extinguisher to review. The design engineer brought a prototype extinguisher to the first meeting and demonstrated how it worked. He also handed out a product specification sheet. Everyone on the team was given an opportunity to operate the extinguisher, and several good questions were asked and answered regarding the similarities to existing models. For example, the product manager demonstrated how the extinguisher worked, highlighting the differences in operation between the new and existing models. One participant asked if this extinguisher would work the same for left- and right-handed people as do the existing models. Another wanted to know the benefits of the rounder shape of the canister.

The team also used the FMEA Team Start-Up Worksheet (see Figure 9.1) as a checklist to make sure they understood their boundaries of freedom and the scope of the project.

Case Study Step 2: Brainstorm Potential Failure Modes

As suggested in the step-by-step FMEA guidelines, rather than dealing with the entire product at once, the team broke analysis of the product design into manageable chunks. The most logical breakdown was into the key components of the extinguisher: the hose, the canister, the charge gauge, and the valve mechanism. The chemical agent in the extinguisher was excluded because another team had included it in an FMEA about six months earlier.

The team then brainstormed all of the potential failures for each of those components. For example, with the hose, potential failures were cracks, holes, and blockages. With the canister, one potential failure was that the canister could be dented, and another was that the label might not be properly glued. They listed the potential failures on the FMEA Analysis Worksheet and grouped them by component (see Figure 9.2).

Case Study Step 3: List Potential Effects of Each Failure Mode

Each failure mode was discussed, and the team agreed on potential effects for each of the failure modes. While there was some disagreement about the likelihood that a certain effect would occur, the team agreed to include all possible effects. Members reasoned that if it was highly unlikely that the failure and effect would occur, then the item would probably get a low RPN anyway.

The team listed each potential effect next to the failure. If members felt that several different effects were possible, and anticipated that each might have a different ranking in at least one of the three ranking categories, they listed them in a separate row.

FMEA Team Start-Up Worksheet		
FMEA Number: 019	Date Started:	March 5
Team	Date Completed:	
Members: Kevin M.	Shane T.	K. C. McG.
Chase L.	Tyler J.	

Leader: Kevin M.

Who will take minutes and maintain records? Shane T.

1. What is the scope of the FMEA? Include a clear definition of the process (PFMEA) of product (DFMEA) to be studied. (Attach the Scope Worksheet.)

This is a design-FMEA to study the new X-1050 model fire extinguisher.

A process-FMEA will be conducted in May.

2. Are all affected areas represented? (circle one)

(YES)   NO   Action: _____

3. Are different levels and types of knowledge represented on the team? (circle one)

(YES)   NO   Action: _____

4. Are customers or suppliers involved? (circle one)   Sales (Chase L.) will

YES   (NO)   Action: represent customers.

Boundaries of Freedom

5. What aspect of the FMEA is the team responsible for? (circle one)

FMEA Analysis   Recommendations for Improvement   (Implementation of Improvements)

6. What is the budget for the FMEA?	$5,000.
7. Does the project have a deadline?	April 15.
8. Do team members have specific time constraints?	Review with steering committee
9. What is the procedure if the team needs to expand beyond these boundaries?	Review with department manager by 3/15
10. How should the FMEA be communicated to others?	Present report upon completion

Figure 9.1   FMEA Team Start-Up Worksheet.

Failure Mode and Effects Analysis Worksheet

Process or Product: Product: Model X-1050 Fire Extinguisher

FMEA Team: Kevin M, Shane T, KC McG, Chase L, Tyler J

Team Leader: Kevin M.

FMEA Number: F019

FMEA Date: (Original) 3/5 (Revised) 5/1

Page: 1 of 1

Line	Component and Function	Potential Failure Mode	Potential Effect(s) of Failure	Severity	Potential Cause(s) of Failure	Occurrence	Current Controls, Prevention	Current Controls, Detection	Detection	RPN	Recommended Action	Responsibility and Target Completion Date	Action Taken	Severity	Occurrence	Detection	RPN
1	Hose; delivers extinguishing agent	Cracks	Misfire	10	Exposure to excessive heat or cold in shipping	5	Insulated pkg mat'ls; temp controlled ship containers	None	6	300	Use hose that is not temperature sensitive	Kevin: 4/1	Changed hose material	10	2	6	120
2		Pinholes	Low discharge pressure	8	Damage to hose during mfg	8	No sharp objects used in operations	None	4	256	Add Protective Kevlar coating to hose	K.C.: 4/15	Added puncture resistant cover for hose	8	5	4	160
3		Blockages	No discharge	10	Foreign object in hose	6	None	Incoming inspect; hose air passage test	3	180	None						
4	Canister; reservoir for extinguishing agent	Paint coverage uneven	Bare spots rust weakening metal; possible explosion	10	Paint line low on paint	6	Automated inventory mgt system	Automated inventory mgt system	2	120	None						
5				10	Spray nozzle partially plugged	9	Regular nozzle cleaning procedure	None	4	360	Keep nozzle in water bath when not in use	Tyler: 3/15	New procedure instituted	10	3	4	120
		Canister dropped			Floor is padded												

#	Process function	Potential failure mode	Potential effect of failure	S	Potential cause	O	Current controls	Detection	D	RPN	Recommended action	Responsibility / date	Action taken	S	O	D	RPN
7		Label not properly applied	Label separates from canister; slips out of hand in use	8	Wrong glue or obsolete glue used	3	Glue standards in place	None	2	48	None						
8		Operating instructions not readable		7	Excessive humidity	5	Climate control in manufacturing facility	Visual	2	70	None						
9	Charge gauge; determine remaining volume of agent	Inaccurate reading	Overfill if gauge reads low; underfill if gauge reads high	10	Gauge not correctly calibrated	7	None	Random calibration inspection	5	350	100% incoming insp.; overflow valve; improve supplier quality	Shane: 4/1	Changed to more reliable supplier	8	4	2	64
10		Broken crystal	Injury to user from cut glass	8	Untempered glass	3	None	Incoming glass breakage test	4	96	None						
11			Injury to user from cut glass	8	Sharp blow to crystal	6	None	Visual	9	432	Use plastic, break-resistant crystal	Shane: 4/1	Switched to plastic crystal	3	3	5	45
12	Valve mechanism; releases agent	Safety pin missing	Extinguisher engages on its own; slow leakage	10	Pin falls out; too small	2	None	Incoming inspection on pin diameter	5	100	None						
13				10	Pin not inserted during manufacturing	9	None	Visual	9	810	Issue pin supply in quantities equal to extinguishers	Tyler: 3/15	Changed mfg. system to issue materials in kits	10	3	3	90
14		Handle jams	User unable to discharge extinguisher	10	Handle becomes rusted	5	Rust inhibitor used	None	7	350	Switch to rust inhibitor preventing metal	Kevin: 4/1	Switched to zinc-plated metal	10	1	3	30
15				10	Spring in handle too tight	2	None	Incoming inspection on springs	4	80	None						

Figure 9.2 FMEA Analysis Worksheet.

Case Study Step 4: Assign a Severity Ranking for Each Effect

Because a failure can have several different effects, and each effect can have a different level of severity associated with it, the team gave each effect its own severity ranking. In most cases, members agreed on the severity ranking, although in a couple of instances they had heated discussions before reaching consensus. In one of those cases, the team could not agree on a ranking and had to hold a vote. Each member voted the score they felt the item should get, and the final ranking was an average of all of the votes.

Case Study Step 5: Assign an Occurrence Ranking for Each Failure Mode

The team began this step by collecting data on failures with similar fire extinguishers. For the failure modes where no data existed, the team identified the potential causes of failure associated with each failure mode. Not only did this information help members determine the likelihood of the failure occurring, but it also helped them target their improvement efforts once they had decided on the items they needed to improve.

Case Study Step 6: Assign a Detection Ranking for Each Failure Mode and/or Effect

The Fire Extinguisher FMEA Team listed all controls currently in place for each of the potential causes of failure or the effect of the failure and then assigned a detection ranking for each item.

Case Study Step 7: Calculate the Risk Priority Number for Each Failure Mode

The RPN was calculated for each potential failure mode by multiplying the severity times the occurrence times the detection ranking. The team noted that there were significant differences among the rankings, which made it easy to distinguish between the items that required action and those that could be left as is. The highest score was 810 points, and the lowest was 48 points.

Case Study Step 8: Prioritize the Failure Modes for Action

One of the team members created a Pareto diagram of the failure modes so that it would be easy to distinguish visually between the items. The team decided it would work on any item that had an RPN of 200 or higher. Two hundred was set as the cutoff point because it encompassed over half of all of the potential failure modes. The team rationalized that an improvement in more than half of the failure modes would be a significant step in the right direction.

With the criteria of an RPN of 200 or higher, there were eight items they would need to attend to.

Case Study Step 9: Take Action to Eliminate or Reduce the High-Risk Failure Modes

Each of the high-risk failure modes was discussed, and the team determined what action would be taken to reduce the risk, assigning responsibility and a target completion date for each failure mode. The target was to have all of the action complete within six weeks, to give the team time to reevaluate the severity, occurrence, and detection of each item, and determine what other work needed to be done before the product introduction date.

Case Study Step 10: Calculate the Resulting RPN as the Failure Modes Are Reduced or Eliminated

After completing the corrective action, the team met, and all members responsible for an action item gave a report. All commitments were met, and the team was able to conduct its reevaluation FMEA at that same meeting.

There were only a couple of cases where severity was reduced, but this did not surprise the team because members knew that severity is the most difficult ranking to impact. In some cases they were able to significantly reduce the occurrence ranking by using mistake-proofing techniques. In others, they improved the detection rankings.

The team's efforts resulted in more than 60 percent reduction in the resulting RPN from the original FMEA total RPN for all items. The eight areas addressed were at or below the target of 200 points. Pleased with the results, team members prepared their final report for management (see Figure 9.2).

Chapter 10

When and Where to Use FMEAs

The FMEA process is widely applicable in a variety of settings beyond the product design and manufacturing processes focused on in this book. FMEAs provide a structure and a common language that can be used by teams in manufacturing and service, profit and not-for-profit, private, public, or governmental organizations. FMEA is not just a tool for the manufacturing or engineering department. It can be used to improve support processes, not just manufacturing processes or product design. A discussion of some of the support processes where FMEA might be useful follows.

Safety

FMEAs were first developed as a tool to identify and correct safety hazards. The FMEA process was developed to anticipate and eliminate safety problems before they occurred. Consequently, FMEAs can be used to improve the safety of the process of manufacturing a product as well as to improve the safety performance of the product itself.

Manufacturing safety FMEAs should be conducted by a team of people who operate the equipment, along with others who are not involved in operating the equipment. This combination of user knowledge and outsider observations provides a comprehensive analysis of the hazards.

FMEAs conducted on products to determine their safety are critical in today's litigious society. Companies have an obligation to assure their customers that their products are safe and fit for use. In many cases, it is not sufficient that product instructions spell out safe operating procedures; safety provisions must be built in to the products. It is helpful to involve consumers or eventual users of the product in such an FMEA. They should be asked to use the product, and other members of the FMEA team should observe how it is used. It is not unusual for a product to be incorrectly used or to be used for an unintended purpose. If these possibilities can be uncovered during an FMEA, safeguards can be built in to the product design.

Accounting/Finance

With some modifications to the ranking scales for severity, occurrence, and detection, FMEAs can be helpful in determining financial strategies and assessing credit or investment risks. For example, before extending substantial credit to a potential customer with a shaky credit history, an FMEA that studies the things that could go wrong with customer credit and how credit failures would affect the company would provide a structure for a credit plan that will reduce financial risk.

Software Design

The effects of software are all around us. Practically everything that we do is governed by software. Software quality assurance is critical in many of these instances. For example, computer systems and the software that drives them are used in air transportation, medicine, and banking, to name a few applications. Problems created by software bugs or incorrect programs can range from nuisances to potentially fatal disasters. As with a product or design FMEA, a software design quality FMEA can identify problems before they occur, so they can be eliminated or reduced.

Information Systems/Technology

Even without software problems, computer glitches can happen because of hardware or systems issues. From the simplest local area network (LAN) to multi-million-dollar telecommunications systems, use of FMEAs can help make both the design and installation of information systems more robust.

Marketing

Billions of dollars are spent on marketing and advertising by U.S. firms annually. Some promotional campaigns are wildly successful, while others are financial busts. An FMEA conducted prior to an advertising or marketing launch can help businesses avoid costly and sometimes embarrassing mistakes. An FMEA can be used to identify offensive or misleading advertising copy. It can also be used to preplan reaction and response to potentially damaging product recalls or disasters.

Human Resources

With organizational restructuring (downsizing, right-sizing), the human resources field is faced with developing and executing plans for new organizational structures that are significantly different from the classic pyramid structures we are all familiar with. Changes on paper that appear to be workable can turn into disasters. An FMEA can be used as a bridge between the plan and the actual restructuring. FMEAs force a structured analysis of problems and glitches that might happen. Plans can be designed to address the potential problems and crises can be avoided, saving time and money while improving morale.

Purchasing

Prior to purchasing a major piece of equipment, an FMEA can be conducted to anticipate problems with different purchase options. This information can be used to improve purchasing decisions as well as to develop installation plans once the equipment is purchased.

Table 10.1 provides specific examples of how FMEAs have been used outside of the design and manufacturing areas.

Table 10.1   Other Uses for FMEAs

Function	Examples
Safety	A plastics molder conducted an FMEA on a new piece of molding equipment to ensure that the safety devices on it worked and that emergency stop buttons were properly placed.
Accounting/finance	A finance department performed an FMEA on its annual budget to make sure it was realistic and accounted for potential emergency expenses.
Software design	A firm that develops CAD software used an FMEA to uncover bugs in the system prior to release for beta testing.
Information systems/technology	The information systems department conducted an FMEA to determine the security of sensitive data.
Marketing	During the development of a new corporate brochure, the marketing department incorporated an FMEA into the design process to reduce the potential of offending potential customers and miscommunicating vital information about the company.
Human resources	An HR department led an FMEA that involved senior managers from all departments during an organizational restructuring.
Purchasing	Working with the process-engineering department, a purchasing group used an FMEA to select a new piece of manufacturing equipment.

Appendix 1

Creating a Process Flowchart

Flowcharts are to manufacturing processes what road maps are to drivers. They provide a detailed view of the process, and increase understanding of how the process flows. With a process flowchart, teams can identify repetitive steps, bottlenecks, and inefficiencies in the process. When used with an FMEA, they increase the team's understanding of the process, which in turn helps the team identify potential failures, effects, and solutions.

The best way to create a flowchart is to walk through the process as if you were the thing being processed or created. The process steps should be followed sequentially, and notes should be taken during the walk-through. Avoid short-cuts while going through the process, as you may miss critical steps.

Once the walk-through is complete, each step should be listed on a self-stick note. It helps to have several people do this, as each will contribute ideas that others missed. The steps should then be grouped and organized according to their order in the process.

For complicated processes with several steps and substeps, it helps to create a top-down flowchart, where each of the major steps in the process are listed in order of flow across the top of the chart, and the substeps are listed underneath each major step (see Figures A1.1 and A1.2).

Once the steps are identified and put in order, symbols are assigned to each step. At this point, missed steps become more obvious and can be added as needed. With all the steps in place, arrows connecting the symbols are added to show the direction of the process flow.

Oval	**Enter and Exit**—Indicates the beginning and ending points of a process flow. All flowcharts have at least one entry and one exit point. There can be more exit points if the process can end at several different points.
Rectangle	**Activity Steps**—Shows activities in the process. There can be more than one arrow coming in but only one arrow going out. Write a brief description of the activity in the rectangle.
Diamond	**Decision Points**—Shows decision points in the process. There must be at least two arrows out of a diamond, and they must be labeled with answers to the questions written in the diamond.
Circle	**Connection**—Used to connect one part of the flowchart to another. The symbols are most often used to connect one page to another in longer flowcharts that extend over several pages. Use letters beginning with A and work through the alphabet.
Double Rectangle	**Major Step**—Identifies the major steps of the process across the top of the flowchart. Breaking a process into major steps simplifies the flowchart and provides a quick overview of the process. The detailed substeps are outlined below each major step.

Figure A1.1   Flowchart Symbols.

As a final step, the flowchart should be tested by walking through the process again, this time using the chart as a guide. Corrections should be made, and a process should be established to review and revise the flowchart periodically to make sure it is kept current.

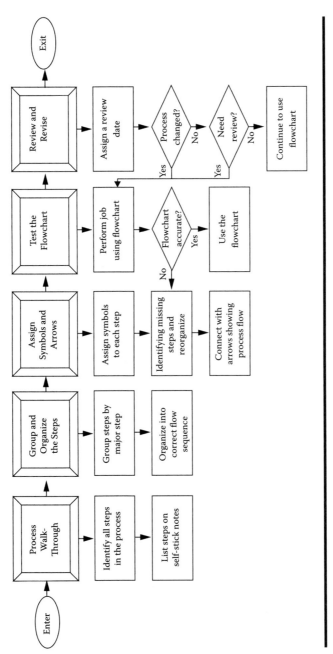

Figure A1.2   Top-Down Flowchart.

Appendix 2

Brainstorming

Brainstorming is a well-known technique for generating a large number of ideas in a short period of time. There are many different ways to brainstorm, depending on the objectives of the session. A round-robin approach works best for FMEAs, because it allows each person the opportunity to express his or her ideas, while keeping the creativity level high.

The round-robin approach to brainstorming allows each person to contribute one idea each time it is his or her turn. Participants should come to the brainstorming meeting with a list of ideas to contribute to the process. New ideas are generated as participants "piggyback," or are inspired by and build on, others' ideas. To encourage creative ideas, no idea should be critiqued or commented on when offered. Each idea should be listed and numbered, exactly as offered, on a flip chart. Expect to generate at least fifty to sixty ideas in a thirty-minute brainstorming session.

It helps to review the rules of round-robin-style brainstorming with the group before the session begins.

Brainstorming Rules

1. Do not comment on, judge, or critique ideas as offered.
2. Encourage creative and offbeat ideas.
3. A large number of ideas is the goal.
4. Evaluate ideas later.

When the brainstorming session is over, the ideas should be reviewed, similar ideas combined, and ideas that do not seem to fit eliminated.

Appendix 3

Reaching Consensus on Severity, Occurrence, and Detection Rankings

Consensus means that all team members can support the team decision. Ideally, everyone on the FMEA team would agree on the severity, occurrence, and detection rankings. In all likelihood, however, there will be some disagreements due to each team member's unique perspective of the process or product. Disagreements without a structured process to address and resolve them can waste a lot of time and energy. The team should agree, in advance, on a process to handle disagreements. Outlined below are some methods to help reach consensus.

Team Voting

Voting and ranking is a vehicle to help the team reach consensus on severity, occurrence, and detection rankings. When there is a disagreement on a ranking, team members who feel strongly about their rankings should present their rationale for the ranking to the rest of the team. If necessary, a time limit (for example, five minutes each) can be put on these presentations. Linking their argument to the predefined ranking scale will help strengthen their position. When the presentations are complete, team members should cast their votes for what they feel the ranking should be. The mean (arithmetic average) ranking should be calculated and used as a reference point for the team to arrive at a consensus score.

It is important not to take the mean score as the "score" without any additional discussion. The voting process is a consensus-reaching tool, but it alone cannot ensure that the entire team supports the ranking.

If the voting process does not help the group arrive at consensus, there are a few other exercises the team can work through to reach agreement.

Get the Process Expert Involved

If the process expert is not on your team, you might want to invite him or her to a meeting to review the FMEA rankings and give an opinion about how the item in question should be rated. The expert should not have the final say in the ranking, but rather should provide the team with information that perhaps they did not know or were not aware of. The team has the final say.

Defer to One of the Team Members

Your team could assign one member of the team to make the final decision if there is a person on the team with a lot of expertise on the product or process. The problem with this approach is that there is a chance some team members might not agree with the ranking and, in turn, will have a difficult time supporting the FMEA from this point on.

Rank Failures and Effects within a Ranking Category

List each failure and effect on a self-stick note. Do not worry about the actual score of the ranking in question. Instead, put the failures in order (from the highest to the lowest) according to the scale in question. For example, if the scale in question is severity and the team is unable to reach agreement on the ranking of two or more of the failure modes, put each of the failure modes on a self-stick note. Then, as a team, put the failure modes in order from the highest severity to the lowest severity. At this point, you should not be concerned with the numerical ranking for the failure modes. Once the failures are in order, indicate the rankings for any of the failure modes that the team has been able to agree upon. By thinking of the failures relative to each other, rather than in terms of an absolute scale, you may be able to agree on the rankings for the failure modes in dispute.

Talking It Out

Because the rankings are multiplied, a 1- or 2-point difference on any one of the ranking scales can have a significant impact on the RPN for the failure mode. The difference could put the item below the cutoff point, when it should be above the cutoff point. This would mean that a relatively high-risk failure would not be eliminated or reduced. Therefore, it is risky to assign rankings arbitrarily just to move the FMEA process along. Sometimes the best way to reach consensus on a particularly sticky issue is to talk it out.

Use the Higher Ranking

If the team just cannot reach consensus, the team might elect to use the higher ranking. The loss with this approach is the time taken away from working on another item. There could be tremendous gains to using this approach and operating on the safe side.

Appendix 4

Examples of Custom Ranking Scales*

Severity: DFMEA Custom Ranking, Customer Satisfaction Examples	
Ranking	Example
10	In-service failure that threatens safety
9	Extensive product recall
8	Unscheduled engine removal
7	Premature (unscheduled) component replacement
6	Oil leak but system still operational
5	Air-conditioning system not operating properly
4	Interior panel rattles
3	Variation in seat colors
2	Door plugs missing
1	Scratch on interior of housing

* Reprinted with permission from the *FMEA Reference Guide* and *FMEA Investigator,* Resource Engineering, Inc.

Severity: DFMEA Custom Ranking, EH&S (Environmental, Health, and Safety) Examples

Ranking	Example
10	Catastrophic product failure causes loss of life or serious injury.
9	Product creates major hazardous environmental disposal problem.
8	Use of product under normal conditions leads to OSHA recordable injury.
7	Use of product under normal conditions leads to exposure above Permissible Exposure Limits (PEL).
6	Product creates moderate hazardous environmental disposal problem.
5	Manufacture of or use of product leads to temporary noncompliance with ISO 14001 audit.
4	Use of product under normal conditions leads to injury requiring first aid.
3	Use of product leads to spill of nonhazardous material.
2	Use of product leads to poor housekeeping.
1	Manufacture or use does not have a detectable impact on EH&S.

Severity: DFMEA Custom Ranking, Event-Based Ranking Examples

Ranking	Example
10	≥5 per design
9	≥2
8	≥1
7	≥1:2 designs
6	≥1:5
5	≥1:10
4	≥1:50
3	≥1:100
2	≥1:250
1	<1:250

Occurrence: DFMEA Custom Ranking, Piece-Based Examples	
Ranking	Example
10	Cpk < 0.33
9	Cpk ≈ 0.33
8	Cpk ≈ 0.67
7	Cpk ≈ 0.83
6	Cpk ≈ 1.00
5	Cpk ≈ 1.17
4	Cpk ≈ 1.33
3	Cpk ≈ 1.67
2	Cpk ≈ 2.00
1	Cpk > 2.00

Detection: DFMEA Custom Ranking, Design Rule Examples

Ranking	Example
10	No design rules used.
9	Design protocols are formalized.
8	Design rules are specified in initial design criteria.
7	Design reviews held to ensure compliance to design rules.
6	Checklist used to ensure design rules are followed.
5	Purchasing systems do not allow selection of nonstandard components.
4	Early supplier involvement so all relevant knowledge about input materials and compliance to design needs are understood.
3	Design software signals compliance issues.
2	Design software ensures compliance to the relevant industry standards.
1	Design software prevents use of nonstandard dimensions, spacing, and tolerances.

Detection: DFMEA Custom Ranking, DFA/DFM (Design for Assembly/Design for Manufacturability) Examples

Ranking	Example
10	No consideration given for DFA/DFM.
9	The number of components has been minimized.
8	Only standard components have been used.
7	Ergonomic assembly techniques have been incorporated.
6	Design elements such as pad sizes, wire gauge, and fasteners have been standardized throughout the design.
5	Modular designs used.
4	Easy-fastening devices (snap fits or quick fastening devices such as quarter-turn screw, twist locks, spring clips, latches) used.
3	Self-testing or self-diagnosis has been built-in.
2	Self-aligning surface, grooves, and guides used.
1	Asymmetrical features used to mistake-proof assembly.

Detection: DFMEA Custom Ranking, Simulations & Verification Testing Examples

Ranking	Example
10	No verification testing used.
9	GO/NOGO tests used to ensure dimensional requirements.
8	Partial functionality of prototype tested before release.
7	Full Alpha tests conducted; no Beta testing.
6	Untested computer model used to simulate product performance.
5	Accelerated life testing of final design before release; lab simulation.
4	Alpha and Beta testing used before release to ensure design meets needs.
3	Product tested for full functionality in customer's application.
2	Finite element analysis to highlight stress concentrations requiring design changes early in the design stages.
1	Computer modeling to ensure form and fit of mating components.

Severity: PFMEA Custom Ranking, Customer Satisfaction Examples

Ranking	Example
10	In-service failure that threatens safety.
9	Extensive product recall.
8	Unscheduled engine removal.
7	Premature (unscheduled) component replacement.
6	Oil leak but system still operational.
5	Air-conditioning system not operating properly.
4	Interior panel rattles.
3	Variation in seat colors.
2	Door plugs missing.
1	Scratch on interior of housing.

Severity: PFMEA Custom Ranking, Operational Examples	
Ranking	**Example**
10	Critical process equipment damaged and unusable or destroyed.
9	Loss of customer due to late delivery.
8	Entire lot of top level assembly product scrapped.
7	Full assembly line (or bottleneck operation) down more than 1 week.
6	Rework full lot of top-level assemblies.
5	Scrap full lot of sub-level assemblies.
4	Technical (engineering) resources required to get line operational.
3	Rework sub-level assemblies off-line.
2	Equipment down for more than 1 hour.
1	Engineering disposition.

Severity: PFMEA Custom Ranking, EH&S (Environmental, Health and Safety) Examples	
Ranking	**Example**
10	Loss of life, serious injury.
9	Large hazardous material spill or release.
8	OSHA recordable injury.
7	Personnel exposure above PEL.
6	Moderate hazardous material spill or release.
5	Fail internal ISO 14001 audit.
4	Injury requiring first aid.
3	Spill of nonhazardous material.
2	Minor (nonhazardous) coolant spill.
1	Poor housekeeping.

Occurrence: PFMEA Custom Ranking, Piece-Based Examples	
Ranking	**Example**
10	Cpk < 0.33
9	Cpk ≈ 0.33
8	Cpk ≈ 0.67
7	Cpk ≈ 0.83
6	Cpk ≈ 1.00
5	Cpk ≈ 1.17
4	Cpk ≈ 1.33
3	Cpk ≈ 1.67
2	Cpk ≈ 2.00
1	Cpk > 2.00

Occurrence: PFMEA Custom Ranking, Event-Based Occurrence Examples (or Examples for Complex Assemblies)	
Ranking	**Example**
10	≥1:2 events (or complex assemblies)
9	≥1:10
8	≥1:25
7	≥1:50
6	≥1:100
5	≥1:500
4	≥1:1,000
3	≥1:5,000
2	≥1:10,000
1	<1:10,000

Occurrence: PFMEA Custom Ranking, Time-Based Examples	
Ranking	**Example**
10	≥1 per occurrence per shift
9	≥1 per occurrence per day
8	≥1 per 2-3 days
7	≥1 per week
6	≥1 per 2 weeks
5	≥1 per month
4	≥1 per quarter
3	≥1 per half-year
2	≥1 per year
1	<1 per 1

Detection (Control): PFMEA Custom Ranking, Mistake-Proofing Examples	
Ranking	**Example**
10	
9	Does not apply.
8	
7	Sensory alert prevention solution; color-coding of drums of raw material.
6	Warning detection solution; audible alarm sounds if overtorque condition is detected with pump.
5	Warning prevention solution; alarm flashes if rate of pump motor torque rise is excessive.
4	Shutdown detection solution; pump shuts down if overtorque condition is detected.
3	Shutdown prevention solution; cycle counter with automated shutdown at MTTF (mean time to failure).
2	Forced control detection solution; automated in-line inspection fixture.
1	Forced control prevention solution; use of asymmetrical features to allow placement of fixture one and only one way.

Detection (Control): PFMEA Custom Ranking, Manual Detection Examples

Ranking	Example
10	No monitoring, measurement, or sampling.
9	Acceptable Quality Level (AQL) sampling plan used for Final Inspection.
8	100% visual inspection.
7	100% visual inspection with visual standards.
6	100% manually inspected using GO/NOGO gauges.
5	Statistical Process Control (SPC) used in-process with Cpk 1.33 or higher.
4	SPC used in-process with Cpk 1.67 or higher.
3	Does not apply.
2	Does not apply.
1	Does not apply.

Detection (Control): PFMEA Custom Ranking, Gauging Examples

Ranking	Example
10	Does not apply.
9	Does not apply.
8	Periodic Non Destructive Testing (NDT).
7	Periodic in-line variable gauging.
6	Periodic in-line GO/NOGO gauging.
5	In-line GO/NOGO gauge on all parts exiting process.
4	Automated inspection on first piece.
3	Dimensions of input materials confirmed with in-process accept/reject gauging.
2	100% automated inspection of 100% of product.
1	Does not apply.

Appendix 5

Process Improvement Techniques

Organizations have a wide variety of approaches to improvement available to them once an improvement opportunity has been identified. The improvement opportunities identified through an FMEA are no exception. Some effective techniques for following through on identified opportunities are described briefly below.

Mistake Proofing

Mistake-proofing techniques, when implemented properly, make it virtually impossible to have a failure. An excellent example of mistake-proofing is a car that will not start unless the clutch pedal is depressed. This prevents the car from lurching forward when it is started. Before this was mistake-proofed, a driver could try to start the car while it was in gear, causing it to jump forward into other cars, objects, and even people.

Mistake-proofing techniques include ways to make it impossible to make mistakes in both the manufacture and use of products. Limit switches, electric eyes, bar coding, and counting techniques can all be used to mistake-proof processes and products.

Examples of mistake-proofing we experience every day include the following:

- Electric heaters that turn off if they fall over
- Car lights that shut off automatically
- Overwrite protection tabs on audio- and videotapes and computer disks
- Irons that shut off after being unused for a set number of minutes
- Automatic seat belts

Design of Experiments

Design of experiments (DOE) is a family of statistical techniques that first help identify the key variables in a process and then determine the optimum processing parameters for the highest quality. Design of experiments is effective in both continuous and discrete processes. DOE can be used in the product development stage as well.

There are many types of DOEs. Full factorials, fractional factorials, response surface methodology, and evolutionary operations (EVOP) are some. Perhaps the most powerful type of DOE is the family of extreme fractional factorial designs called screening experiments.

Using a screening experiment, it is possible to vary several process variables at the same time and statistically determine which variables or combination of variables have the greatest impact on the process outcomes. Once these key variables are known, the FMEA team can focus its efforts just on these variables, saving time, effort, and money.

Statistical Process Control

Statistical process control (SPC), another statistical technique, is a tool that can be used to monitor processes to make sure they have not changed or to compare the output of a process to the specification. One SPC technique, control charting, enables operators to monitor key process variables and adjust the process when it changes, before it goes out of control and produces a bad product.

The FMEA team can use control charts to get a real-time view of the process. When a failure occurs in the process, the control charts will signal a change. By quickly reacting to the signal, the team can work to find the root cause of the failure before the trail gets cold. Once the root cause is found, mistake-proofing can be used to eliminate the failure mode, taking the resulting RPN to essentially zero.

Team Problem Solving Using CI Tools

Many processes and products can be improved using basic continuous improvement (CI) tools and the brain power of the improvement team. Basic well-known improvement tools include brainstorming, flowcharting, data collection and analysis, voting and ranking, Pareto analysis, cause-and-effect analysis, and action planning.

Appendix 6

ISO/TS 16949 Requirements Referencing FMEAs

ISO/TS 16949 is the quality standard for the automotive industry. It is based on ISO 9000 and builds on QS-9000, which was the quality systems requirement originally developed by the Chrysler/Ford/General Motors Supplier Quality Requirements Task Force. Their goal was to develop a fundamental quality system that provides for continuous improvement, emphasizing defect prevention and the reduction of waste in the supply chain. ISO/TS 16949 incorporates a process approach to the quality system requirements originally presented in QS-9000.

The requirements of Section 7.3 of ISO/TS 16949, "Design and Development," include product and manufacturing process design and development. The standard focuses on error prevention rather than detection and specifies the use of FMEAs as part of this effort. Specific clauses citing use of FMEA include:

7.3.1.1 *Multidisciplinary approach*

The organization shall use a multidisciplinary approach to prepare for product realization, including

- development/finalization and monitoring of special characteristics,
- development and review of FMEAs, including actions to reduce potential risks, and
- development and review of control plans.

7.3.2.3 *Special characteristics*

The organization shall identify special characteristics [see 7.3.3 d)] and

- include all special characteristics in the control plan,
- comply with customer-specified definitions and symbols, and
- identify process control documents including drawings, FMEAs, control plans, and operator instructions with the customer's special characteristic symbol or the organization's equivalent symbol or notation to include those process steps that affect special characteristics.

Note: Special characteristics can include product characteristics and process parameters.

7.3.3.1 *Product design outputs—Supplemental*

The product design output shall be expressed in terms that can be verified and validated against product design input requirements.

The product design output shall include

- design FMEA, reliability results,
- product special characteristics and specifications,
- product error-proofing, as appropriate,
- product definition including drawings or mathematically based data,
- product design reviews results, and
- diagnostic guidelines where applicable.

7.3.3.2 *Manufacturing process design output*

The manufacturing process design output shall be expressed in terms that can be verified against manufacturing process design input requirements and validated.

The manufacturing process design output shall include

- specifications and drawings,
- manufacturing process flow chart/layout,
- manufacturing process FMEAs,
- control plan (see 7.5.1.1),
- work instructions,
- process approval acceptance criteria,
- data for quality, reliability, maintainability and measurability,

- results of error-proofing activities, as appropriate, and
- methods of rapid detection and feedback of product/manufacturing process nonconformities.

Section 7.5, "Production and service provision," focuses on the require-ment to plan and carry out production and services under controlled conditions through use of a documented control plan. References to FMEAs follow:

7.5.1.1 Control plan

The organization shall

- develop control plans (see annex A) at the system, subsystem, component and/or material level for the product supplied, including those for processes producing bulk materials as well as parts, and
- have a control plan for pre-launch and production that takes into account the design FMEA and manufacturing process FMEA outputs.

The control plan shall

- list the controls used for the manufacturing process control,
- include methods for monitoring of control exercised over special characteristics (see 7.3.2.3) defined by both the customer and the organization,
- include the customer-required information, if any, and
- initiate the specified reaction plan (see 8.2.3.1) when the process becomes unstable or not statistically capable.

Control plans shall be reviewed and updated when any change occurs affecting product, manufacturing process, measurement, logistics, supply sources or FMEA (see 7.1.4).

Note: Section 7.1.4 relates to change control.

Reprinted from *ISO/TS 16949:2002 Manual* with permission of the International Automotive Task Force. For more information contact AIAG (www.aiag.org).

Appendix 7

Alternative FMEA Worksheets

The Fourth Edition (2008) of the Potential Failure Mode and Effects Analysis Manual (by DaimlerChrysler, Ford and GM Supplier Quality Requirements Task Force) introduced alternative formats for the Design FMEA and Process FMEA Worksheets. Alternative worksheets are included as Table A7.1 (Alternative Design FMEA Worksheet) and Table A7.2 (Alternative Process FMEA Worksheet) annotated with a brief explanation of the major (optional) changes.

Table A.7.1 Alternative Design FMEA Worksheet

Design Failure Mode and Effects Analysis Worksheet (Alternative Version: major changes noted.)

Product: _____

DFMEA Core Team: _____

Team Leader: _____

Model Year/Program: _____

Design Responsibility: _____

DFMEA Number: _____

DFMEA Date: (Original _____

(Revised _____

Page: _____ of _____

Item (Component) and Function	Requirement	Potential Failure Mode	Potential Effect(s) of Failure	Severity	Classification	Potential Cause(s) of Failure	Current Design Controls, Prevention	Occurrence	Current Design Controls, Detection	Detection	RPN	Recommended Action	Responsibility and Target Completion Date	Action Taken and Completion Date	Severity	Occurrence	Detection	RPN

DFMEA Analysis Results — *Current Design* — *Action Results*

An optional column, requirements can be used to augment analysis of a specific failure mode.

The Classification column can be used to highlight high priority failure modes and/or to classify special characteristics.

In this version of the worksheet, the Occurrence Ranking has been moved after the "Prevention Controls" column to recognize that the Occurrence Rankings can be affected by prevention controls.

Table A.7.2   Alternative Process FMEA Worksheet

Process Failure Mode and Effects Analysis Worksheet (Alternative Version: major changes noted.)

Process: _____

Model Year/Program: _____

PFMEA Core Team: _____

PFMEA Number: _____

Team Leader: _____

Process Responsibility: _____

PFMEA Date: (Original) _____

(Revised) _____

Page: _____ of _____

Process Step (Component) and Function	Requirement	Potential Failure Mode	Potential Effect(s) of Failure	Severity	Classification	Potential Cause(s) of Failure	Current Controls, Prevention	Occurrence	Current Controls, Detection	Detection	RPN	Recommended Action	Responsibility and Target Completion Date	Action Taken and Completion Date	Severity	Occurrence	Detection	RPN

PFMEA Analysis Results

Current Process

Action Results

Requirements are the inputs to the process specified to meet the intent of the design and/or customer needs.

The Classification column can be used to highlight high priority failure modes and/or to classify special characteristics.

In this version of the worksheet, the Occurrence Ranking has been moved after the "Prevention Controls" column to recognize that the Occurrence Rankings can be affected by prevention controls.

FMEA Glossary of Terms

AIAG: Automotive Industry Action Group.

Design of experiments (DOE): Series of statistical techniques used to introduce controlled change into a process and to study the effect of the change on the process outcomes.

Detection: FMEA ranking scale that defines the likelihood of detecting a failure or the effect of the failure before it occurs.

FMEA: Failure Mode and Effect Analysis. A systematic, structured approach to process improvement in the design and process development stage.

ISO 9000: International quality standards for product design, manufacture, and distribution.

Mistake-proofing: Making the process so robust that it cannot fail; also called error-proofing.

Occurrence: FMEA ranking scale that defines the frequency of a failure mode.

QS-9000: Automotive sector-specific quality requirements made optional with the introduction of ISO/TS 16949.

Resulting RPN: Risk priority number of a failure mode and its corresponding effects after improvements.

Risk priority number (RPN): Risk priority number of a failure mode and its effects before improvement.

Severity: FMEA ranking scale that defines the seriousness and severity of the effect of the failure, should it occur.

Statistical process control (SPC): Statistical technique used to monitor processes, usually involving the use of control charts.

Total RPN: Calculated by adding together all of the risk priority numbers for an FMEA. This number alone is meaningless, but can serve as a gauge to compare the revised total RPN once the recommended actions have been instituted.

TS 16949: Also known as ISO/TS 16949, this standard is based on ISO 9001 but contains complementary automotive industry-specific requirements adding to the standard both a process orientation and a focus on the customer.

Index